Angels in Pinafores

Alice Lee Humphreys

ANGELS IN PINAFORES

John Knox Press

RICHMOND · VIRGINIA

Ninth printing 1971

Copyright, 1954, by John Knox Press, Richmond, Virginia
Printed in the United States of America
Library of Congress Catalog Card Number: 53-11764
International Standard Book Number: 0-8042-2256-8

TO

Dr. and Mrs. Archer Le Roy Smethers

They are Angels of God, in disguise;
His sunlight still sleeps in their tresses,
His glory still shines in their eyes.

From "The Children," by Charles Monroe Dickinson

Contents

Angels in Pinafores

INNOCENCE, INC.

*L*ATELY, I did christen my First
Grade Schoolroom, Innocence, Inc. For behold, at every Check-up
of Assets, I am newly amazed at the utter Guilelessness of Six-
Year-Olds. Yea, and how the tiny members of the Corporation,
though all diverse, do so Unanimously Tick.

Now, schoolteaching is no Frolic. For Children do not come
Pre-packaged as sweetcakes or rolls. Nevertheless, as Chief
Adviser, I view a unique organization where the alien elements
of Doubt and Worry have never entered. Likewise, where all
groups make beguiling contributions, each after its Own Kind.

The controlling personnel at School's beginning are what
might be termed, The Over-Steppers. Ignorant of all Property
Bounds, these tiny Innocents do busily notch tables or whittle
chairs. They strip tinfoil from candy bars or crunch apples with
unreluctant appetites. Bereft at first of Speech, they do sit with
feet elevated on their own chairseats—their knees on a level
with their heads. Whereupon, if I gaze reprovingly upon them,
they do, without one trace of guilt, look Straight Back!

But Shyness doth not long freeze the lips of Innocence,
Inc. Suddenly there is a great Thaw. Then do the Optimistic
Palaverers take over. The task of this committee is to Shine up
Life because it is so Dreadful Nice. Once I did watch them

originate a game called, What I See. One emboldened Lad shut his eyes for concentration, and after ruffling up his shock of red hair, saith with mock belligerence, I see a Billygoat with long horns coming down the road. But this pessimism was scotched by a little Maiden of equal imagination who chirped confidently, The horns of that Billygoat are not for Hooking. I saw him take one off, and he just Blowed it! In such fashion Optimism aboundeth within a First Grade Classroom. On the drabest day, the Palaverers are wont to burst into high trills and crescendos over a murmuring shell or a strange bright feather. These tiny Fledglings, so lately removed from the Source of All Happiness, know not the meaning of a Low Mood or a Black Friday. But in the cloudiest weather, they do ever maintain a continuous, twittering Jubilance.

Hardly, however, have I become accustomed to their bubbling hilarity, before The Astonishers crowd my horizon. So baffling and unpredictable is this committee that it succeeds in keeping me from foreseeing the Shape of any new day. When I asked Hilda the condition of her grievously ill Grandfather, she made this surprising deduction, He is worser. Now they are afraid he can't Last until the End! But Hilda's ability to Amaze was equally manifest in Rolfe. When I requested my cocksure Lad to repeat our newly memorized Bible verse, The Lord loveth a cheerful giver, Rolfe brought forth this astounding version: God loveth a chicken liver. Another seasoned Astonisher was tender-hearted Brenda. With hot tears in her eyes, she did lash out against a certain Institution, thus: I think it's a shame to call a place for little Orphans, The Odd Fellows' Home.

Beloved, as you have surmised, there is no Monotony within the confines of Innocence, Inc. For behold, by the time I have recovered from the stimulation of The Astonishers, I am assailed by their near Kinsmen, The Phrase-Turners. These original Twisters of Words show a genius beyond their mere Five-and-One Years. Later will they assume the thoughts and mannerisms of Grown-ups. But now their chief purpose seemeth the taking of Starch from a Teacher's Conceit. Well do I remember thanking Mary Elizabeth for a slice of her birthday cake only to hear her answer with sweet graciousness, Oh, I did it just for Charity. Albeit, the most unusual Variation was uttered by Andrew, Driver of Hard Bargains. Lisped this shrewd, tongue-tied Trader, dangling a glass marble before the unsuspecting eyes of a wristwatch owner, I'll Chade even. I'll Cheat You Right.

But the largest Constituency of Innocence, Inc. are the Candid-Cameramen. Having taken the Teacher for Better or Worse, these sober-truthed Officials do it with disarming honesty. Dickie, during a certain recitation, did fix his eyes upon me with flattering intensity. Being ignorant, I took this as a citation for good teaching. But he deflated mine Ego by pointing to my new red smock and exclaiming excitedly, It is just like the Elephant Man's at the circus! His tablemate was as transparently Sincere. One morning for her sentence prayer, Claudia did bow her shining head, fold her dimpled hands over her stomach, and murmur in a low, reverent tone, Every time I am sent to the board to Write, I want to Draw. Confused? Nay, these Children live in a world in which they quip and wonder—but the Right of which they never question.

Transcending all other groups, however, are the Spiritually-sensitive Little Ones known as The Sages. Beneath their elusive smiles, lieth a store of unshakable Faith hidden from the skeptical hearts of Adults. What Grown-up ever marvelled over the condition of the world during the three days following the Crucifixion? My Fant did. Saith he dreamily one Easter Season, as he watched the new-born daffodils flaming on the school walk, God must have taken Good Care of us during those three days when Jesus was in the grave and couldn't. Or what Seer could have explained with Barbara's fine discernment, this goodly reason why Christ did not turn the Stones into Bread? Barbara confided with touching conviction, His Father had something better for Jesus than plain Stone-bread. He wanted to give Him a real Feast with Angels as Waitresses.

It is these Mystical and Unworldly qualities which have ever proclaimed Little Children as true Ambassadors to the Kingdom of Heaven. Yea, and it is such memories which are my Yearly Dividend from Innocence, Inc. Without them, teaching school would be one Long Drought followed by Lean Seasons of Rationing. I would remember only the daily Grind and Toll of Energy. Or minor irritations like Fist-fights, Dribblings of Paints, and the bathing away from my fingers of such unwanted gifts as ticklish Worms and June bugs.

Wherefore, when I now take Inventory, I strive to number the eager, shining faces. Likewise, the sensitive mouths from which issue such surprising Pronouncements. And all other seductive Chit-chat, accompanied by tiny feet keeping Jig-time. Moreover, I confess to an Empty Feeling as the word Retirement looms nearer. And I pray that when I can no longer Shepherd my Little Ones, I may still borrow enough Rosiness from them to give Warmth and Spice unto my Latter Days. Yea, and that I may be permitted to keep my Remaining Interests within the exciting, whimsical, indescribable, and wholly undefinable circumference of Innocence, Incorporated!

H E was trial-sized, snub-nosed and tousle-haired. And he had remained after School to help me put materials in their rightful places. This he did, not from a sense of Duty, but of Delight.

And it came to pass after I had thanked him, that he departed not. But he stood with little fat hands bunched within his sweater pockets, gazing upon me with curious intensity.

What wantest thou? questioned I wearily. And he answered shrewdly, Why do not thine own Little Boys come to help thee after the school day as do the Sons of the Other First Grade Teacher?

And I answered with great Assurance, God giveth little Lads and Damsels only unto Married Persons. Then (mayhap because I had on this same day removed the first gray hair from mine head) I did add defensively, Now I am still Swift of Foot, yet am I unmarried.

At this admission, was the Lad astonished beyond measure. His mouth, which habitually did tilt upwards at the corners, now rounded in incredulity. Stepping closer, he took a new and fuller Inventory. Verily, he did weigh me with his penetrating Gaze. Then with sober judiciousness, gave he this Decree:

WELL, I GUESS IT'S TOO LATE NOW!

At this refreshing Candour, laughed I unto Exhaustion. Yet for reasons of mine own, determined I to keep this Pleasantry unto myself. And behold, at that moment there came into my schoolroom, the Well-favored Young Teacher of the Fourth Grade. And she demanded the reason of mine Hilarity. And I answered, There is something which I deemed hidden even from the Wise and Prudent. And lo, it hath been revealed unto Babes.

And when she entreated me further, then did I relate the whole occurrence. And she was convulsed likewise. But she took out her Compact and gazed long at her image. Then she saith, That was an huge Brickbat for you to receive at a School Day's end.

Nay, I replied, sometimes I like Factual Speaking. Lately, have I somewhat against these Adults, who at Social or Civic Clubs do address me and my Contemporaries as: Girls. Such veneering of the Truth never faileth to convince me that I am truly a Museum Piece.

Well, contended the Young Teacher, still gazing into her Mirror, did not the Lad's words have a like effect?

Nay, I declared, the remembrance of that Innocent Quip will be as Youthening unto me as a trip unto my Beautician. For as often as I re-live that ludicrous moment, that often shall I feel the tense muscles around mine eyes and corrugated brow relaxing. Thus at the price of no Shekels whatsoever, my Countenance shall be Rejuvenated, and my Spirit of Youth renewed!

BLUEPRINT OF THE
GOLDEN RULE

*T*HERE was one Perry, a volatile Madcap, numbered amongst us. And so despitefully did he use everyone within his radius, that the fear of his Anger was upon us all.

Moreover, was he without excuse save for this reason: He was the possessor of a Surname which was a constant source of Shame and Ridicule. Wherefore, during school hours sat he in an unhappy state of Self-consciousness. But once on the playground, Perry did hunch his shoulders and hitch up his tiny trousers in an effort to bolster his Inferiority Complex with Aggression.

Thus, his approach to the grounds was a virtual Call to Arms. Small of stature, he would jump high in the air to reach taller Opponents. While resting between bouts, his blue eyes flashed with a steely, combustible quality, as with his boot toe he did trip innocent Passers-by or fling their caps to the ground.

Now, all of this Cross-fire might have been averted by merely changing the Suggestive Surname by law unto one of Honour. But the Lad's Father felt no concern over the matter. Wherefore was I daily in a state of Indecision, pondering thusly: Shall I chastise or shall I Forbear? If I resorted to the former, Perry repented not. While if, in using the latter, I said with restrained patience, Perry, why art thou such a Fighter? he would reply with forced bravado and clenched fists: I juster am.

Thus it happened on a March day when the restless wind fidgeted within the bones of Perry, that he encountered our Eunice on the outside steps. Now Eunice was clad in a white Angora beret with spotless mittens of the same and a matching white Muff. And the unhappy Lad in clothes which smelled neither of Myrrh nor Aloes, did resent the clean daintiness of the little Damsel. Wherefore made he havock of the Muff, striking it from her hands to the muddy ground.

And lo, as I hastened to execute the Fierceness of mine Anger, Eunice came unto me in a breathless little half-run. And she was untouched by the Indignity. Instead, gave she the Defiant Lad a look in which Reproof and Pity were mingled. Verily, in that moment the Six-year-old Damsel sensed the Inseparable Oneness of Mankind. For she spake twelve words, which if followed by Christians, would hasten the Kingdom. Stroking the soiled Muff, she said unto me in her low, Responsible Manner:

Sometime, I must take a day off and tell him about God.

QUEEN FOR A YEAR

*B*EHOLD, I met the New Teacher from mine own school upon the streets. And she saith, Turn aside, I pray thee, for a little space. And I said, We will do even so. Then as we sat us down on an iron bench of the Plaza, she confessed forlornly, I am consumed with Loneliness. For in mine own small village, it hath ever been the custom to salute all Newcomers in the Marketplace. Here, ended she in trembling voice, I am truly accounted a Stranger.

And straightway I determined to turn her aside from Home-sickness, saying, This is my Coronation Day. Dost thou not see how the very grass of the Plaza doth bow and flutter?

Now the New Teacher answered never a word. But her look said eloquently, How cometh it that Trustees of this school do employ a Subject fit for a Mental Institution?

And I ignored the inference, saying, Always in September a Crown is set upon mine head. A Coronet which I may wear for the nine months making a School year.

Then begged the New Teacher earnestly, Speak not to me in Riddles.

So said I plainly, When I first came unto this City, I too was aware of the veiled and chilling glances of Strangers. But on the third day, heard I a high, piping voice shouting the length of the block, Hello, Teacher! And lo, as I walked farther, there assailed mine ears a squeal of excitement, Mother, yonder goeth my Teacher! In like fashion was I acknowledged from store counters and bus windows. So did the Children set the object of their loyalty before the Publick in a most conspicuous way. But the Publick stared in disbelief, that so unlikely a Subject should gain Royal Acclaim.

Here paused I to gaze at my Companion. And lo, she was still discomforted. So I spake on, saying, Within the schoolroom my prestige did still enfold me. Ever and anon, was a recitation interrupted by voices saying, Yesterday, saw we thee upon the streets. And their tones implied Awe and Sovereignty as though they said, Yesterday, saw we the Queen!

A tiny smile flickered over the face of the New Teacher. And she inquired, How fareth it with thee during Summer Vacation?

Alas, confessed I, at that season am I an Expatriate. Suspended are the cheers. Verily, the Children whom I have taught now gaze at me as at a Fossil, saying, Art thou *still* teaching?

At last, the New Teacher laughed outright. So with boldness I ended, When the month of September draweth near, then become I again the Heir Apparent. The eyes of First Grade Applicants burn their Lights of Anticipation when I meet them in the Marketplace. Moreover, I hear Mothers whispering unto them with craftiness, Speak unto this Lady. She may be thy Teacher. And they speak not. But they gaze shyly in Awareness, judging me with their candid, innocent eyes. Then doth mine Ego begin to strut. Blind am I unto the sea of indifferent, Adult faces on the whirling tide of the streets. Instead, I look across unto this Plaza where the grass doth flutter and make Obeisance.

That soundeth poetic, saith the New Teacher, but wherein may I hope for Comfort?

And I answered, Because that on the Queenship no one holdeth a monopoly. Yea, always when I see a New Teacher, young in years but wretched with Homesickness, then long I to say, Forbear a little longer, my Beloved. For behold, thou too shalt walk in Honour. With the affirmations of thy Little Ones enfolding thee, thou shalt soon feel the Royal Insignia emblazoned on thy chest. Yea, and hear an invisible flourish of Trumpets proclaiming thee, Queen for the Coming Year!

DONNA

EVER was I aware of what Sin I had committed. But Once Upon the First Day of School, I had what is known as an Observer. And behold, this Student Teacher stayed until dismissal hour, taking notes of all that was said and done. And ever and anon she did upbraid me with her eyes. For she was possessed of Many Methods.

Whereupon, said I unto her at day's end, It is written upon thy countenance that something in my manner of Teaching hath offended thee. Speak, I pray thee, with Candour.

Then did the Young Observer vacuum her notebook with thoroughness. And she saith indulgently, There seemed to be perfect Correlation in thine Orientation Program save in thy reading of Comics at Story Hour. With such abundance of good Literature, I marvelled that thou didst digress in such fashion.

Wherefore explained I, Four years ago, began I a new School Session with renewed Self-Esteem. Had I not, at a Summer School, gained all Knowledge of Methods?

Hence launched I an Acquaintance Period. And I introduced my Little Ones to everything from their Cloakroom Hooks unto the Janitor's Furnace. And behold, at the first day's end, they were wearied, insomuch that some slipped from their chairs to doze upon the floor.

But one little Maiden, named Donna, sat upright with alertness. To me, she resembled a Canary. For she was sprightly and clothed in yellow. Yea, even the buttons on her sweater were of a shining golden hue.

And straightway she arose, and sidling up to me, she joggled mine elbow. Then she lifted incredibly blue eyes unto mine in immediate friendliness. In her hands, held she a much-folded paper. And at once I knew it to be what is commonly termed a Funny Paper. And she saith maturely, This morning had I no time for reading Bugs Bunny. Then leaned she contentedly against me for better listening.

But alas, I glanced at my Plans for the day, and saw that they were good. Wherefore, warded I off her intrusion, saying, Another time will I read The Comicks.

On the second day, the little Maiden ventured again unto my side with her sheet of Pink. And I said with a great Show of Patience, Did not thy Mother read this unto thee last evening? And she replied earnestly, But I wanted thee and the Children to hear also. Then used I Over-virtuous Tones, saying, That is praiseworthy. Put it into my desk drawer. And behold, at a convenient season will I read it unto all.

Now on the third day, Donna sat gravely in her place, her little ankles crossed in Propriety, her hands folded in her lap. Once seemed she about to speak. But she only gazed from me unto the desk drawer in wistful expectancy.

At this point in my recital unto the Observer, was I forced to pause. For a vast lump was gathering in my throat. Albeit I was able to end with seeming composure, Thus did Donna pass out of my room on that day. And never saw I her again.

The Student Teacher was unimpressed. Did she move unto another school? asked she, fluffing out her hair. Nay, I answered. That night had she an Emergency Operation. And she never awoke from the Anesthesia.

At last was the Observer stirred. How dreadful! saith she in true Sympathy. Then did something deep within me whisper, Mayhap now is the time to show her that in Teaching, one must dilute Exactness and exalt Understanding. Wherefore said I, Thus was school ended for Donna in three days. And in my Remorse, all detailed Plans did appear Foolishness. Especially when I considered how my little Maiden now had Knowledge of the Universe. Yea, and of Eternity.

Since then, ended I, on every first day of school all the weary Little Ones sit on the rug and delight in hearing Bugs Bunny. And in imagination, Donna is always beside me . . . one hand twisting the golden buttons on her sweater, the other resting in trusting fashion on mine arm.

Oh! exclaimed the Observer with new Discernment. It would not have mattered in a day, or even a month, if, for a Child's Pleasure, thou hadst forfeited a moment of thy Program.

I nodded agreement. And together we bent over the paper which Donna, after the manner of Children, had folded into a tiny square. And I knew the Observer was seeing not only the Anticks of Bugs Bunny, but a small Maiden with defenseless eyes of blue. Whilst deep from mine own heart arose the silent, oft-repeated question, Donna, art thou Listening?

PRAYER SIREN

ACH day at the twelfth hour, a loud Whistle calleth our city to Prayer. During that moment of silence, all souls are supposed to utter a petition for our Men in Uniform. Yea, and for Peace throughout the World.

Now, my Little Ones sometimes disregard my calls to Duty. But of the Prayer Siren, make they a Ritual. Verily, I often wonder as I gaze upon the bowed heads and whispering lips what measures of Faith and Trust their hearts do utter. But of the compelling Whistle (I speak to my shame) I am often oblivious.

Thus, it fell out one noon as I wrestled with school supplies in a closet, that I suddenly became aware of a deep and unnatural Silence. The Jungle of Sounds had ceased. For one moment I held my peace, revelling in the magical stillness.

Then there came unto mine ears the sound of stealthy tiptoeing. Turning mine head cautiously, I beheld Jerry, surnamed The Teller, advancing in my direction. In spite of his reverential mien, well knew I that he was bursting at the seams with Information. For one dramatic moment paused he in the closet doorway, placing his hands on his little spare hips with Authority. Then he spake, emphasizing each word separately, and using the rebuking tones of a Mother calling a tardy child to dinner:

Prayers Is Ready!

TEARS, IDLE TEARS

F ever I do stand accused before a Court, then may Patrick be a One-Man Jury. For he possesseth the uncanny ability of overlooking all Human Imperfections.

Yea, he is continually beseeching me for his Classmates. If it be so small an offense as some Child's Tardiness, then from beyond my rebuke do I hear Patrick's reassuring voice saying, Perhaps he had to wait for his Hot Cakes this morning. These Alibis are ever rising to the schoolroom's surface. But the Lad's overflowing Compassion did reach its maximum in the Case of Lucy.

This Damsel was dissolved in tears for the space of four-and-one weeks of school. My more Unfeeling Little Ones did label her, Cry-Baby. But certain others, catching the contagion, did change her woeful Solo into a Quartet of Weeping.

Then indeed did mine own forbearance become dulled. Especially when I learned through the Grapevine Route that Lucy had been promised a Pony if she attended school. Yea, and that she continued to cry the more, hoping to hasten the arrival of her Prize.

Thus, on a day when her Outcries had been perpetually before us, I said desperately (and more for Rhetorical Effect than otherwise), Woe is Me! Doth anyone in this room know the reason for Lucy's new Lamentation?

And immediately Patrick reached across the aisle and handed the Weeping Niobe a clean tissue. And he gazed upon her awhile with musing tenderness. Then he lifted his deep blue eyes unto mine in entreaty. And he spake that which remaineth for me unto this day the classic example of Poetic Chivalry:

Her Tears lie Close to her Eyes!

RAMBUNCTIOUS RIB

*T*ODAY, my First Grade did use the last five minutes of school for dramatizing what they termed, Good-by to the Garden of Eden.

According to the Eternal Fitness of Things, they chose Maria as Eve. For this Maiden is the most beguiling person in the room, daily wearing scarlet-tipped fingers and peeping from behind them in provocative fashion at the school's young and well-favoured Principal.

The Adam selected was the most self-effacing Lad of the group. When Maria beckoned unto him to come forward, he wriggled in Embarrassment, clumping and shuffling to an imaginary stage. There he stood breathing with difficulty and twitching his feet.

Now it was fully understood that the Action must begin at the Departure from Eden. Nevertheless, Eve could not refrain from first dashing into the Supply Room, there to drape herself in some discarded lace curtains. Drawing her cloke of Covetousness around her, she advanced with boldness, abandoning herself to the joy of the Temptation. Regaining the stage, she fluffed out her tangerine-colored curls and called to a thin, ill-favoured Lad: Be the Snake. To Adam, she added with imperiousness, Say something concerning the Apple.

But, alas, Adam had no gift for Improvisation. Moreover, he was so overcome with Shyness that at first he could only stand there reddening and swallowing alternately. Finally, however, he did awaken unto the earnest proddings of Eve. Gazing downward he saith shamefacedly, That was the best Apple I ever et!

At this unexpected turn in events, my small Cloud of Witnesses were convulsed. But Eve was complacent. Reinforced by Adam's half-hearted co-operation, she toyed happily with his statement concerning the Delectable Apple. Then suddenly she pushed the Snake forward and opened an imaginary Gate. One could feel the Tragedy gaining suspense as she paused dramatically and glanced backward for a last Assessment of Eden.

Here was I forced to intervene. Thou art sent from the beautiful Garden forever, I did remind her. However, if thou art truly sorry, there is One who will care for, and protect thee.

Wherefore did Eve gaze at the hard New World awaiting her. Mistaking the meaning of my prompting, she saith blithely unto Adam, There goes the Snake before us crawling on his tummy. That is good. He will scare away all who would hurt us.

Here, happily the dismissal bell ended the Drama. As Maria discarded her Fripperies, an inner voice did remind me, And not Maria only. Verily, some of the Adult Daughters of Eve do appear to trust in the Wiles of Satan rather than in the Protection of God. Yea, there be a few, who through Diplomacy and Cunning, do still remain the most unruly Ribs of the Sons of Men.

THE PLACE WHEREON
THOU STANDEST

*T*IPPIE hath a Vital Personality. As she walketh Up and Down the schoolroom or goeth To and Fro upon it, she doth Twist and Side-step. And when she entereth each morning, she precipitateth herself upon me, Skidding herself to a Stop.

Yet a fortnight ago, she did suddenly become afflicted with a Checkmate. That morning as I spake of God's Presence, and of His being closer than Hands and Feet, Tippie, overflowing with high spirits, came rollicking in.

Then happened the curious Phenomenon. All of the other First Graders betook themselves unto their several tables. But Tippie hovered over my chair. The Gravity of her Situation was apparent on her expressive little face. Moreover, as she put her foot forward for her first step, she did halt, bracing herself carefully. Finally, however, she gained her table, stepping all the while as gingerly as though treading on fragile shells.

At first, marvelled I with great wonderment concerning what Childish Phantasy the little Maiden celebrated. Then was I stricken with grave concern over her Loss of Locomotion. And I questioned her anxiously, saying, Art thou ill? Then beholding the glow of health upon her cheeks, relapsed I sharply into Modern Parlance, demanding, Tippie, what is thy Big Idea?

Her first words fluttered and died away within her throat. Then flushing and twisting uneasily, she raised troubled eyes unto mine, saying with compassion,

I'm afraid I'll Step on God!

FULL OF LAUGH

HE maple tree beyond mine apartment window bent obligingly unto the Autumn Wind. But behold, when she lifted her head, all of her remaining leaves lay scattered on the ground in yellow and orange Glory.

Then sighed I in distressful manner. For I was wrestling over Report Cards, and October had disturbed the rhythm of my work. Yea, the bare branches of the maple tree had minded me of the empty report card of Benjy.

This same Benjy lived a Pantomime Existence. For the space of the first twenty-and-eight days of school he had vouchsafed neither an Aye nor a Nay. Too shy to trust his tongue, his sole communication had been a low Grunt to express disapproval or content.

Possessing my Soul in Patience, I restrained my Natural Impulses concerning Benjy. But the sight of his bleak report card now forced me to new tactics. I determined to seek out his Habitation and receive from his Mother some method for loosening the Portals of his Speech.

And lo, when I reached my journey's end, the entire Family were assembled on the tumble-down porch smiling their greetings. The rotund little Mother waddled down the steps, her fat face illumined in a good-natured glow. Then suddenly, like unto an unpredictable Bolt of Lightning, Benjy bounded in a gallop from the cabin. At first his mouth fell open in Astonishment, for he wist not who had come thither. Then a timid, elusive Grin did appear. This, tried he to suppress, placing his hands against his mouth to hold in the Laughter. But a trickle of Merriment came from behind the hand, choked but infectious. Then began Benjy to whirl round and round, finally throwing himself on the piazza floor and abandoning all Reticence in an uncontrollable spasm of Laughter.

Now that the Spell of Silence was broken, hysteria caught the whole Assemblage like a strong, tidal wave. Benjy's Father did slap his thighs and roar in imitation of Gabriel on the Last Day. The Children, likewise, squealed and rolled on the floor. The obese body of the Mother shook until it did literally spill over with Merriment. Finally, she pleaded pantingly, Hush, Benjy! I'm so full of Laugh that my inside fixin's is strangling me.

As for mine own self, I surrendered also unto the same happy state of Effervescence. Yea, it was the maddest, merriest moment I had ever experienced. As I held out mine hand weakly in farewell, the Mother, still bubbling over, explained, Benjy had near 'bout give you out. I figger that when he seed you actual at the door, hit were such a Pleasurement he couldn't hold in no longer. She paused breathlessly, ending with a note of earnestness beneath her irrepressibly high spirits, Hit were sech an Obligement to him fer you to come.

And, indeed, from that moment some hard obstruction seemed to dissolve within Benjy. The next morning, he had found the Longitude and Latitude of School. With unbridled tongue spake he unto the Children. Moreover, at the hour of reading he did perform another Miracle. Peering over my shoulder, he whispered with correctness the words missed by his Fellows, proving that during his seeming Absence from Learning, he had possessed interested eyes and ears.

In such fashion was the knotty problem of Benjy solved. And his previous state was no marvel. For hitherto had he known only a household of Easy Laughter. Accustomed to this perennial Freshet of Mirth, he had been stricken dumb by the serious, studious countenances of his Schoolmates. It had taken only a visit of Friendship, plus some uninhibited Laughter, to initiate him into the Routine of School.

Such simple advances still remain a great Obligement to all the Benjys in their Wary, Timorous World.

A SONG IN THE NIGHT

F Successes there be divers kinds. But this I never realized until mine Unambitious Allan did manufacture Loveliness out of Pain.

In truth, this easy-going Pupil took liberties with Knowledge. Untroubled by Too Much Thought, he strove to hide his ignorance by blithe chirps of Singing. So irritating became these Eruptions that I upbraided him continually, saying, It will take more than a Ditty to promote thee unto the Honourable Man thou shalt some day become.

Then would his loud Proclamations change unto low, incessant Hummings. But I was not hoodwinked. Well knew I that Allan would ever have one more Song. And this he did unconsciously, without malicious intent. If perchance I kept him after school to show how he might study without Benefit of Song, he forebore his piping with agreeableness. Nevertheless, as he departed, would he begin to Hum from sheer joy of freedom. Then would ensue this dialogue:

Allan, art thou Singing again?

Yessum.

Didst thou know that it had begun anew?

Nosum.

In such manner admonished I him, little recking the Sequence soon to follow.

It happened a week after Vacation was begun that Allan, while climbing a tree, did lose his footing and crash downward upon a large Terra-cotta. Yea, so terrific was the fall, that the lines of the earthen pipe were imprinted upon his tiny stomach.

Moreover, it transpired that during his stay in the Hospital, I was there as a patient likewise. And my room was over against Allan's. And it was a time of oppressive heat. Yet the greater part of my suffering resulted from the hearing, through the doorway, of my Lad's constant Groanings. Verily during the long days and nights of his outcries, I was remorseful in that I had ever deemed his singing Offensive.

Then one night, at the hour when Human Life flickers lowest, there floated down the stifling corridors the sound of a Child's voice raised in Song. It was Allan's. Awaking without pain, he was warbling in his high sweet treble, the old-time favorite, Jingle Bells. With startling distinctness drifted the words through windows and open doorways:

Dashing through the snow
In a one-horse open sleigh . . .

Then the Miracle did happen. On that memory-laden tune, a new Season came into the hearts of the Listeners. Breaths of frosty air seemed to sweep through the torrid halls. Memories of Winter Nights drifted through Private Rooms and Wards alike. The nurses declared that faces began lighting up and tense nerves relaxing. A veritable Epidemic of Optimism followed. It was the Contagion of Christmas Enchantment. One quavering voice joined Allan's. Others followed until a great company of the Bed-ridden were contributing to that ancient melody of Goodwill.

Now, I lay there shaken with Happiness. And I thought of other Melodists whom God had used for His Night Songs. Of Paul and Silas singing in the Philippian Jail while their falling chains made fit accompaniment to their Paean of Rejoicing.

And I remembered how, in these Latter Days, so often there is no Signpost indicating the Gift a Lad or Maiden will make to the Future. And I promised myself never again to be dismayed. But to say instead, Let no one call any Child hopeless. For I have witnessed the Tribulations of Humanity beguiled by a carefree Lad's Musick. Verily, have I seen mine own Irresponsible Allan take a vast Accumulation of Pain and make it Sing!

FLUTE AND DRUM

ONCERNING Musick, Carolyn is a Responsive Instrument. But her voice, high and silver-toned as a Flute, doth not fall into the Limited Niche demanded by the Score. Verily, transcending all Bounds, it springeth upward like unto a Fountain. Leaving my other Vocalists on their prescribed lower notes, this small Melodist straineth her Capacity and in heady flight Soareth away.

Now it came to pass that I heard Carolyn conferring with my unfortunate Basso, Benson, concerning their Inadequacy in Musick. And behold, Benson's confidence was Impaired. For the Supervisor had tested the Lad's voice concerning Pitch and Tone, and Benson knew of what Sort it was. But Carolyn had a Fixed Believing. Shaking her curly pate at the Somber Lad, she piped encouragingly, My Mother liketh your singing, Benson. She saith that it soundeth like a Bass Drum. Or the Great Organ with all the Stops Out!

For a moment, Benson considered this hopefully. Then remembering the perfectly attuned First Grade Choir, he did shake his head disconsolately, saying, It hurts my Face to try. But Carolyn, during this revealing period, was to be neither Baffled nor Belittled. Giving Benson a regal nod, she saith with Bland Assurance,

I useter could Sing good before they Made Tunes.

$\mathcal{I}$T was a Picture-card Christmas miraculously compounded of sleet, ice, and snow.

Against this magical world of white stood small, unyielding Clara. Her back was turned to the fairy-like fretwork of Frost on the window. Yet was she as a flaming candle upon that Yuletide sill. Yea, her topaz-colored eyes did give off Sparks. And her fierce little red topknot shook defiantly.

For Clara of a surety expected Santa Claus to visit us on this eve of the holidays. And now that the time was fully come, two of mine older and more worldly-wise Lads did taunt her saying, Thou wilt have no guest today, Clara. And they waxed mightier in Unbelief, ending, We have known for many months that there is no such man as a Santa Claus.

But Clara, unmoved by this devastating statement, kept herself under dignified control. If that be true, saith she with inescapable logic, why then did the Postmaster mail my letter, licking a stamp thereon?

At this crucial moment, the Ethiopian Janitor raised his voice in conciliatory tones, saying, Firm yourself, Honey. You is keyed up too high. You is bound to come down.

But Clara, buoyed by her own outburst of Faith, was deaf to all disenchantment. Lifting her assertive little nose higher, she rustled her green taffeta skirt with greater Authority. And to me she resembled naught so much as a tiny outraged hen with ruffled feathers.

Meantime, the snow piled higher against the windows and the silence down the ice-rimmed road grew deeper. Listening in sore distress to the clock ticking nearer to school's end, I knew that Clara was likewise approaching the last of her resources. But not until she cried out to me in desperate earnestness, saying, Tell them that Santa is a Really-man, did I know of a certainty that she had reached her last Citadel.

And instantly my mind did perform a flash-back. Yea, I was remembering a phone call made the evening before unto mine Aunt. In bitterness had I stated my dilemma concerning Clara. And, I ended, I have invoked and supplicated but no Santa Claus is forthcoming. No, not even his suit of clothes.

Then spake mine Aunt soothingly, saying, Have Patience. Trust thou a little further in the unforeseen workings of Providence. And I flung up the receiver, laughing her to scorn.

But now, twenty-and-four hours later, I was rebuked and brought back to the present by the faces of my Little Ones. For with one accord were they gazing at Clara in trusting hopefulness. And I found myself praying earnestly, Please, God, let it come true.

Then from weakness (speak I to my shame) resorted I to the Tactic of Evasion. And I spake unto the Children saying, Mayhap a Traffic-jam of Snow hath prevented Santa. Lo, since fifteen minutes only remain, thou, Clara, mayest dispense the Fruits and Candies for our party.

Whereupon, the little Damsel struck a Napoleonic attitude. Folding her arms boldly across her chest she saith with certainty, We can wait longer. It will taste better from Santa's own hands.

Suddenly she paused, tilting her head to listen. For lo, from somewhere in that snowy expanse had sounded the muffled strugglings of an automobile. When the rumblings became too audible to be mistaken for fancy, I said disconsolately within myself, It is merely some Parent coming before dismissal. For I dared not to hope.

But my pessimism touched not the hearts of my Little Ones. Throughout the room, like a high charge of electricity, ran an air of Joyful Expectancy.

Then a car stopped at the schoolhouse. And some darted from their tables in a whirlwind of happiness. They heard the sound of a door slamming and the crunching of footsteps on snow. During the brief pause which did follow, neither I nor my Children seemed to breathe. Neither could we speak nor move when a single pressure of the knob opened the door.

And now, stupefaction turned into amazed delight. A whisker-less Santa did stand before us clad in the apparel of a woman. The robe enfolding her was of scarlet satin, and her belt was a green cord from which tiny crystal bells chimed and jangled. She wore a curly wig of silver. And above it, she had tilted a red cap adorned with holly.

At sight of Mrs. Santa Claus, I felt a surge of infinite relief. Gratefully advanced I to greet her but she saluted me not. Neither gave she any sign of Recognition. Instead, she saith in a sonorous voice, I fain would speak unto a Maiden whose name is Clara. For lo, Santa Claus hath sent me in answer to her letter.

For a long moment, Clara stood transfixed with happiness. Then with a high little sob which was also a half laugh, she did throw herself headlong into Mrs. Claus' arms. With quick exploring fingers touched she the cheeks reddened by wind and snow. Finding they were real, she spake with the directness of a six-year-old, saying, I knew You Would Happen! Then she leaned contentedly against the ample bosom, taking swift inventory of the visitor's basket.

By now, all of mine other Lads and Maidens had joined Clara under her Faith Banner. That is, all save the Two Doubters, who believed yet hid their faces and trembled.

Then from the schoolroom arose sounds of childish wonder mingled with high little grace notes of happiness. Likewise, a sweet savour ascended from the basket. As I smelled thereof, the years did roll backward. And I was a child again eating cookies made after this same manner in mine Aunt's own Kitchen. Small cakes were they topped with caraway seed, the whole melting in one's mouth from the pure creaminess thereof. Other cakes had she fashioned into angels, with wings of silvered paper.

Today, as my Children did crunch upon these cakes of like design, saw I that the Lads did crumple the silver wings in their pocket for keeping. But my little Damsels pinned them with delight in their curls. Verily, Mrs. Claus and the Children did have a Love Feast interrupted too quickly by the dismissal bell.

Then passed Mrs. Santa Claus with alacrity through the doorway. In vain did I beseech her, saying, Hold me no longer as a Stranger. But she answered me nothing. Instead she did catch the hand of Clara, allowing the little Maiden to walk by her side to the car. As the two disappeared in the snow-filled yard,

I knew that the taffeta skirt of mine high-spirited Damsel was rustling with renewed Importance of Authority.

Late that evening spake I again into the telephone. And I said unto mine Aunt, I am still lightheaded over the coming of Mrs. Santa. Then added I, That Merry Dame hath visited mine apartment also. Behold, I found my treasured housecoat of quilted satin spread on a chair for drying. And one curl from her wig saw I upon the floor.

Then did mine Aunt break her long silence. And she said, Beloved, the Faith which doth remove Mountains must ever be an Adventure beyond things one can see. Keep thou the curl as a memento of a child's Faith which surpassed thine own.

And so I did. Verily, unto this day have I that silvery curl. And it is a testimonial of Clara's unquenchable Belief. For while it did not remove Mountains, it did entice the First Lady of the Northland from the Pole!

PART-TIME ANGEL

IVE-YEAR-OLD Roberta it was who daily furnished me with six hours of Nurse-maiding, and her Grade with Surprises and Merriment. Verily, she rationed not her Mischief. For Roberta was Spacious-hearted.

Nevertheless, mine heart was suddenly smitten one morning when I considered how all meaning of Concentration lay still beyond the little Damsel's Ken. Wherefore paused I in the day's Program, suggesting, Let us repeat a poem especially for our Roberta. And we spake in Choral Fashion the old Nursery Rime: Where art thou Going, my Pretty Maid? And we ended, My Face is my Fortune, Sir, she said.

And Roberta heard us gladly, regarding us with an expression of beatitude strangely mixed with Subtilty.

At recess hour, we were scarce gone outside when I missed Roberta. Moreover, I was unsurprised to find her within the dusty confines of the Cloak Room. For this stale, unheated spot regarded by Adults as little better than a Mausoleum hath to Children of all ages ever been Enticing Territory.

Once within this Sanctuary, Roberta had, for her own accommodation, dragged my chair before a small wall Mirror. By her side was a Kit of Cosmeticks likewise belonging unto her teacher. In all directions for a distance of two cubits, Fluffs of Powder lay like a light snow upon the floor. In her hands, which still bore the ten Dimples of Babyhood, held she a jar of Foundation Cream and a Lipstick. And her face, possessed naturally of rose-petal texture, now with its smears of red and white, was the grotesque image of a tiny Clown.

As I entered, she was discoursing flippantly with herself. But I heard only the word, Fortune. For I was wroth, considering mine own wasted shekels and the Damsel's lack of fresh air. Prim-lipped, asked I in stern reproof, What in the world art thou doing here?

Roberta hadn't expected Reproaches. This personal adornment, deemed she the Ultimate in Taste and Judgment. Wherefore looked she up with a roguish grin on the painted lips. Giving a vain tilt of her blonde head, she spake with Simplicity this Profound Utterance:

I be puttin' Cream and Lipstick on my Fortune.

ONE WHO WAS LOST

*I*T happened on a bitter January day at an earlier-than-usual dismissal hour. Afterwards, I learned that from babyhood my mischievous Judy had ever loved Disappearing Scenes with their after-effect of Shock and Audience Reaction.

But this, her most startling and terrifying Dramatization, I shall always remember Photographically. One moment, my schoolroom alight with gayly chattering little Creatures eager to be off. Then somewhere between the Adieux and the home welcomes, the Losing of Judy.

Her Mother, coming at the usual closing time, did find the schoolhouse locked and the yards deserted. Then repaired she unto the abodes of Kinsfolk and Acquaintances. Finally, when she inquired at my door, three hours had passed away. And I knew there was cause for Haste and Effort.

Yet concealed I my mounting uneasiness, saying, Behold, a list of the street addresses of my entire Grade. When thou hast found into which of these abodes Judy hath made one of her frolicksome Side-Dashes, do thou call me upon the Telephone.

And as the Mother drove away with the Speed of Jehu, I did rush privily to inquire of the hospitals concerning Accident Cases. Yea, and with heavier Forebodings obtained I the Janitor's Key and did search the many schoolrooms. And the Basement also. For by now grim possibilities were clutching at my heart.

And lo, as the afternoon grew apace, the distraught Mother returned, saying, It seemeth as though the Earth hath swallowed up my Child. And she started out a-fresh, her Objective being the sixteen furlongs of Highway lying between the School and her Country Abode. This road, saith she bravely, will I Police— for sooner or later will Judy return the one way Home. But unspoken between us lay terrifying words like Cruising Taxis, Pick-ups, and Kidnappers.

Now the next two hours did constitute for me a Lifetime. Yea, because of them, never shall I hear the Parable of the Lost Sheep without an indescribable Tightening of the Throat. My whole World came to a Standstill. It seemed to be holding its very Breath waiting for Judy. Above, the sky was gray and inscrutable. While the January Wind sweeping through the bare trees' branches, made them appear as sinister arms reaching.

Nor were these the only Modes of Self-torture. My Conscience was smitten with many trivial Recollections: Of Judy's voice with its amused and reckless Good-morrows, and her beautiful blue eyes which resembled dewy cornflowers. Likewise, was I stabbed with the remembrance that her Father was a Marine fighting even now for the Safety of his little Maiden. Further-more, I could imagine his Accusation, She was loaned unto you to be watched and guarded over.

To escape such mental Torture, repaired I unto the home of a dear Friend. And the two of us phoned continuously for any possible Clue. And the Friend saith consolingly, Somewhere the Venturesome Little Imp is hiding happily. And behold, if I were her Mother, when she did appear, then would mine hands not Slacken.

But I answered, Thou knowest not the Weight of Responsibility which hovers forever over the Head of a Teacher. Furthermore, if the Damsel be not found by morning, then shall I be committed for Safe Keeping within a State Institution.

Wherefore my Friend, albeit as fearful as I, laughed me to Scorn, saying, From thee have I learned that School Teaching is a Life-long Emotion. And she ended with an hollow attempt at Raillery, Surely whenever one of your profession enters the Better Land, there is a special Fanfare in Heaven!

But I rebuked her saying, Cease at this time from Levity. Then began the clock to strike the hour. And behold, Twilight began to settle over the World. Rushing again unto the phone, I prayed earnestly as I gave Judy's number. There was first an agonizing Silence. Then heard I the voice of the Mother in joyful assertion, A moment ago the gate did click. And lo, through the Dusk beheld I Judy coming up the walk.

Now for Pure Joy said she no more. But later learned I that the Little Prodigal had no explanation save that when she grew weary from walking, she had rested within some Woods, hiding when she heard her Mother's call because she dreaded the Aftermath of her Folly. And she had fallen into her Mother's arms, her breath coming in jerky gasps, the dead leaves of the Forest clinging to her honey-colored hair.

Now with the joyful Words of the Telephone dancing round and round within my brain, my blood likewise began to pound as an Engine in mine ears. Light-headedly, glanced I beyond the windows. And lo, all Nature had relented also. The restless Wind was still, and the bare limbs of the Trees reached no longer.

Then arose I and journeyed toward mine own Abode. And my Feet seemed to be saying, Thank Thee, God, in a ceaseless Rhythm of Gratitude. I heard my Friend call from afar, Rest now. Thou art Dead on thy Feet. But I answered extravagantly, Nay, I shall never be weary again!

Now, such thought I to be the Truth. But I had lived an Eternity within those Six Agonizing Hours. Wherefore, my Knees did suddenly begin to sway beneath me. And as I reached my rooms, I was as Breathless and Spent as a Runner.

And verily, I had Run a long distance. Yea, all the way Home with Judy.

NOT TO THE SWIFT

THE Mountain Peaks lay wrapped in fog. And as Mincie entered school, her hair was pearled with dew.

As usual, she was Tardy. Nevertheless, she seated herself in the number circle, Remote and Unapologetic. Striving to reach the impenetrable brain behind those shrewd, calculating eyes, I said casually, Mincie, is it raining?

Her eyes expressed all the Bewildering Enigma that was Mincie. Yea, and the inscrutable Fastnesses of her Hills.

No, she saith stolidly. Hit's jest Mistifying.

Now concerning all Mathematics, I possess a large Endowment of Folly. Moreover, on this particular day, I was weary of watching the monotonous counting of sticks, marbles, and even grains of corn to establish a Concept of Numbers. Wherefore suggested I unto the First Graders, Let us for Pure Fun, count unto a Hundred.

This feat, knew I, to be truly done, must be performed as an Entirety. If one Halt or Break occurreth during the Recital, lo, the whole Pattern doth Dissolve.

So as a further means of Testing, I added, Let us not always begin at the Number 1. Perchance Mincie can start counting at 29.

With a Closed Look, the little Damsel began to stroke the red gingham dress which at so few points did touch her thin body. Then she gazed at me as though I had proposed a Revolutionary Act. However, from her low Muttering of Numbers, could I tell that she was bestowing much labor upon reaching 29.

Mincie, prodded I sharply, in this Game, you must instantly begin counting at 29.

Tarnation! drawled my Mountain Maiden in tones as aloof as the peaks surrounding us, I got to Git Thar Fust!

Now some Wise Person hath said that Slow Growth is one of the Great Economies of God. Mincie expressed this, only in terser Fashion. Verily, since that day, never have I beheld a Caterpillar forced from its Cocoon, a Chick from its imprisoning Shell, or an Immature Child struggling with Problems far beyond its Ability, that I am not warned by Mincie's Unvarnished Reproof.

True, I taught her little. But from her did I learn that All Things, before their Appointed Unfolding, must needs Git Thar Fust!

THE DICTIONARY WORD

HEN my Lads feel the first grass of Spring between their toes, then do they begin to hurdle Restrictions. Yea, if Authority be not high, they sometimes express this seasonal waywardness upon an Individual.

Now on a windy, aggressive day in April, I beheld such a Company. And they were a-straddle a piece of iron piping which their imagination had transformed into a Mule Train. Moreover, they were drifting unto a corner of the playground where my Lad, Daniel, stood in a solitary space apart.

And the Company's Leader, being a Bargainer, straightened himself until his little round stomach protruded like a balloon. And he spake unto Dan in lordly fashion, saying, In the Teacher's presence, thou art our Pal. But thou canst never be on this Mule Train until thou answereth this question: Why doth thy Mother never give us Surprise Treats as do the other Mothers of this school?

Then did Daniel of the sober face and hungry heart, reinforce himself against the playground fence. And he saith quietly, My Mother hath a very serious Illness of Beauty.

When he had spoken thus, then were his Tormenters skeptical. And they compassed him round about, and tantalized him further, chanting, Dan's Ma hath an illness. And the Leader spake a second time, clenching his fist and saying, What *is* this Beauty Illness?

Verily, the Leader's sharp tongue had touched the raw places of Daniel's soul. But the Lad only smiled a slow-breaking smile. And he saith with quiet triumph, It is a Dictionary Word.

And suddenly, the entire Corps had respect unto Daniel's utterance. The word, Dictionary, had produced an Awe almost mounting unto Envy. Yea, even the Leader's little balloon-shaped stomach became deflated as he questioned with grudging respect, *What* word?

Then did Daniel's face become strangely illuminated. Seeing its steadfast glow, I thought within myself, Only in the face of a Child is Loyalty ever so written. And he said in a forgiving rush of confidence, Beyond the door of my Mother's room, heard I two doctors talking. And one said unto the other, This is plainly the case of a Too Beautiful Neurotic.

The Leader was uncomprehending, but impressed. That is tough, declared he sympathetically. And straightway abandoning his own place on the iron piping, he said magnanimously, Thou canst be Lead Mule.

In the throes of a happy trance did Daniel take the place of honor on the Mule Train. Miraculously enough, the Elements calmed. Albeit a capricious wind threw down a chaplet of tassels from the alder tree upon the Lead Mule's fair head. Forgetting his loneliness, his feet raced round and round the playground with Pegasus-like swiftness. His heart had a bursting feeling as though it contained more happiness than it could hold. And he shook the tassels from his blonde hair in an ecstasy of Delight.

THUS SAITH THE TEACHER

*T*HE day was far spent when I saluted the Mother of Yannis in the marketplace. Her dark eyes were sparkling with Animation. And as is her custom, she began to throw her native Greek into English at a charming and breath-taking rate.

Mine leetle Yannis, saith she, he ees two year beyond thee now in School Grades. Still remembers he much unforgettable things you did teach. Every day or so he ees speaking them to me. She caught her breath, ending with a veritable Explosion of Gratitude, Eet ees hard to eggsblain how much we two value them so high to each other.

Now the school day had worn deep Lines of Servitude upon my brow. Wherefore reasoned I, Perchance it will prove exhilarating to hear from the Mother of Yannis how I commanded the attention of her Lad by some Grace of Speech. Verily, argued I further, if I appropriate this Praise, then will I have somewhat to think upon during the Lean Years. So I spake desirously, saying, Tell me what things I unwittingly gave unto Yannis for Remembrance.

Then answered the irresistible little Greek Mother, Eet ees thoughts put in a new manner from the Greek. She struggled awhile with her acquired English, finally relying on vivacious gestures to surmount the Barriers of Speech. And I warned myself inwardly, saying, Do not let this Flattery plug thine ears to the truth. Still I could refrain no longer from wondering what inspiring words of mine had lived on in the heart of Yannis.

It was the Lad's Mother who brought me out of this vainglorious reverie. One thing you spake was thees, saith she, folding her arms with a Teacher's Confidence. Then she pursed her lips with the Precision of one Summarizing, and spake Academically:

Well, So much for That!

Thus was I dashed from my Pinnacle of Self-esteem, in all innocence by the Mother of Yannis. Albeit, so human and hungry lives the heart of a Teacher that I could feel a fresh flush of Anticipation. Yea, and a renewed Stiffening of my chagrined Spirit. And I said hopefully within myself, Mayhap in Yannis' second Remembrance, my Life Efforts have flowered into some Perfect Work. Therefore spake I with alacrity, Say on!

The Mother of Yannis nodded her head agreeably, adding obediently, Then will I Say!

Depending again on Pantomime, she snapped her fingers to indicate an Instructor's High Disdain. And she uttered with Old-world Charm, this Absurdity of which I am often guilty:

Feedle-Steeks!

Not soon thereafter did I rejoice in Utterances from mine own Tongue. Rather, a verse of Scripture haunted me continually. And the Burden of its Request seemed peculiarly mine own:

Set a Watch, O Lord, before my mouth: Keep the door of my Lips.

BEHOLD, THIS DREAMER
COMETH

A Non-conforming Child is a Reproach unto any Teacher. But mine (save for Conscience' sake) is my daily source of Refreshment.

This Roddy, a slender Lad of Elfin features, turneth school into a Daydream Session. Mine other Pranksters have books to make them wise. But this Child sitteth remote from their bustling activities, moving freely in the World of the Spirit.

If it be true that There is a Divinity which shapeth our Ends, then in Roddy possess I a Poet or some sort of Scientific Genius. For this Child hath a mighty Spirit of Discernment. During the few moments allotted my Pupils each day for describing beautiful things on the way to school, the Literal Ones exclaim with great admiration concerning gaudy Roadside Advertisements. But my Dreamer showeth the perception of a Millay. As an example, when Autumn doth drop her red and gold Greeting Cards, he exclaimeth excitedly, Today, saw I a Sun-setter Tree! Or on a misty Winter's morning as he gazeth toward the hills, he is wont to say regretfully, There's not much to see. The mountains are wearing Veils on their Faces. And in Spring, he once joyfully beheld a Little White Snowdrop come Quivering Up!

With all these things is he endlessly diverted. But he feeleth Lassoed at school. Yea, even as he gazeth respectfully at me enduring the punishment meted out during quarter-hour lessons, he hath already yielded himself unto Dreams. And he cometh to life only when Dismissal Bell soundeth.

It was inevitable then that a day should arrive when I needs must Keep Roddy In. And behold, when it came, he did perform all the mechanical tasks his fellows had accomplished during school hours. This he did without complaint. Albeit, it was an Abomination unto him until he made a startling Discovery. Teacher, deducteth he triumphantly, the word Look always weareth a Pair of Glasses!

But I was weary and I did admonish him sternly, saying, Thou shouldest be talking of thy New Beginnings. Yea, and thy need for a Goal. And I waited. But Roddy contributed nothing. Then suddenly outside on the fragile pattern of pale blue sky, a black velvet Butterfly with traceries of gold did drift lazily past the window. And my Lad was transported. Opening unto me like a shy flower, he saith raptly, Yea, let us talk. Let us talk about what maketh the Starch in Butterfly Wings.

Thus daily, and in such unpredictable ways, it hath become apparent that Roddy will never keep books of Profit and Loss. And the thought pricketh mine heart. For I remember the sight of the Adult Sons-of-Rest on the benches of small-town squares, endlessly whittling, and swapping Idle Tales. And it frighteneth me to recollect how many of these men were once, like Roddy, possessors of Many Talents. And I find myself wondering if he, like they, will have to surrender high Aspirations because he faileth to Focus on any one Goal.

Howbeit, in spite of Omens, still labour I hopefully for a Miracle. And I strive to find some well-defined, reliable path by which my Will-o'-the-Wisp may follow visions unto their successful Reality. Yet all the time some Absurdity within me whispereth that whatsoever this Lad attaineth, he will gain in sudden Heady Flight . . . while the others Trundle along Laboriously.

After all, there be other measures of Success than Stocks and Stones. Who knoweth? The time will probably come when I shall proudly claim a Listener's part in these days when my Little Visionary opened his heart concerning Butterfly Wings, or the beguiling Veils on the faces of Mountains. Of two things, at least, am I positive: That God hath entrusted one of His Higher Dreams unto Roddy. And that even He will have to become resigned unto a long Period of Waiting.

In the meantime, others may own all of the Realities, but Roddy will possess the Graces!

CONSPIRACY

*T*HE Blustering Voice on the telephone was that of Jesse's Father. Jesse, he boomed, hath defied me concerning the taking of his medicine. And lo, the Little Exhibitionist hath crawled under our abode unto a spot where the flooring almost toucheth the ground. Then the voice of this man with the stature of a wrestler, did suddenly betray the Stamina of Mush. And he ended on a lame, frustrated note, We want you to hasten over and Make him come out!

Then replied I dubiously, This *Make* Business hath never succeeded even within the Bosom of my schoolroom. Nevertheless I will come.

Hastily, I pushed through the dividing hedge. With no sign unto the Parents, I gat me down on All-fours, and crawled under Jesse's habitation. There waited I silently lest haply the small Culprit manoeuvre backwards and never be able to extricate himself.

As soon as mine eyes were accustomed unto the darkness, I espied Jesse. Like a tiny inscrutable Buddha squatted he within a narrow, shadowy area, giving the appearance of being wedged within his Shrine.

Uttering a prayer that I might not startle him unto a lower, more airless retreat, I forced my voice unto a half-whisper, saying: Jesse!

For one moment the Little Buddha remained motionless. Then unto mine utter surprise, he advanced toward Life-giving Air and Roominess. Yet from the curiosity so transparent on his face, knew I that the Truce had not been effected from a sense of Obedience. Rather, gathered I that my Secretive Air and Undignified Creeping Position had given the transaction quite a Clandestine Meaning.

With a cautious whisper exactly duplicating mine own, he saith in the tones of a Fellow Conspirator,

Teacher, is he after *You*, too?

POTATO BUG

Unto me, his Teacher, Joseph's
Imagination merely had Periods of Flight. But unto the General
Publick, he was an outrageous mixture of Ananias, Dr. Jekyl,
and Mr. Hyde.

Not that the mind within his tow-head was mediocre. His
gayly Embroidered Tales were so intriguing that even his Schoolmates were envious. Verily, when he strained their capacity for
Belief, they only raised indulgent eyebrows, asking hopefully,
Joseph, did it truly happen? And the Little Fibber would give
them a regal nod, asserting, Just ask Potato Bug.

Potato Bug was the Imaginary Playfellow whom he had framed
and brought to Life. An entrancing Mythical Lad of extravagant
Physique. One who could perform all the Feats of Courage
which Joseph, being small of stature, could not accomplish.
Even this impossible fabrication did possess the full flavour of
Truthfulness:

My friend Potato Bug, saith Joseph with assurance, can train
Pigs. And behold, each morning before daybreak, he sendeth
one of his pigs unto me on a tricycle to deliver the mail.

By now, was my patience wearing thin. Moreover, this last
Fable furnished an opening wedge. So I rebuked him severely,
saying, Joseph, hast thou checked with thy Conscience to see
whether a Pig be mailman on thy street?

The sly Prevaricator appeared to consider this suggestion. Then answered he with his usual boasting, Thou canst ask Potato Bug.

That I shall do, replied I, pressing my point. Lo, this very afternoon thou shalt show me thy Pig Trainer.

Here was an unsettling situation. Nevertheless Joseph had to accept the Inevitable. And lo, when I repaired unto his abode, he first of all dismissed his Mother. Then went we, the two of us together, into the garden. And we spent a long while gazing at Nothing. Whereupon, Joseph was of a sad visage. And I said, Why is thy Countenance fallen? And he replied, Because thou canst not see Potato Bug.

Then I, not wishing to deprive him wholly of the Gift of Imagination, did refrain from saying, Potato Bug is a total Fraud. Instead I replied tersely, It is even as thou sayest. Thine own Teacher cannot see Potato Bug.

But these disillusioning words seemed only to renew his enthusiasm. For lo, his Fancy did take another Imaginary Leap. Pointing excitedly unto the same blank spot, he exclaimed triumphantly, There goeth Potato Bug! And he ended in admiring tones, That boy sure can Cover Ground!

Now, I am aware that many a Lonely Child goeth places in Imagination with an Unseen Companion. Albeit, as Joseph passed upward through school, I did question his teachers and learned with happiness that he Improvised no longer.

Moreover, in the end, I did behold Potato Bug. And it happened on this wise: When Joseph reached the age of eighteen years, he joined himself unto his Country's Army. And a few months later, he did win the Silver Star for bravery in Korean fighting. And I was in his home town at the Presentation Ceremony. And lo, Joseph had become an humble Lad. And he stirred uneasily at the well-deserved Praise.

Then, after the High Command was departed, I did add mine own congratulations. But the one-time Braggart dismissed it all in matter-of-fact tones, saying, It was nothing.

Yet probed I further, asking, Dost thou still remember the Double-life thou didst pursue in my First Grade?

And Joseph laughed guiltily. And he saith blushingly, I believe that was because I was such a Scrawny, Pint-sized little Scamp!

Nay, replied I, and at last I have something for the Psychologists. And because he looked mystified, I added, In Potato Bug, thou didst almost erase thine own Identity. Yet the Germ of the Hero was ever in thee crying for expression. And lo, it hath now blossomed into a Star for Gallant Action.

And I could not refrain from adding, Yea, today I do confess that I never expected this triumphant sight of Potato Bug. And I touched his shining Star, ending with a laugh which would not keep steady, No, nor had I any idea how heroically, in Korea, he would Cover Ground!

KEEPING IN SHAPE

During the War Years, many secret shadows crossed mine heart. For numbers of Servicemen did bring unto me their First-Born. And they charged me with much tenderness concerning them. Moreover, some of these Fathers never returned . . . and one of them was Roberta's.

For the space of several months, none of Roberta's classmates believed that she had been told of the Loss befalling her. And they had reason. For she persisted in uttering a Sentence Prayer at Devotional each morning. And always it ended thusly: God bless my Daddy, too. Amen.

Therefore, when she had made an end of speaking, certain of my Children did pass wise and patronizing glances in her direction. But I, being her teacher, was not deceived. For although Roberta maintained her Serenity, nevertheless I had seen quivering waves of Recollection sweep over her sensitive little face.

Once it happened when a shaft of early sunlight filled the school doorway. Glancing up, I caught its reflection in the eyes of the tiny Five-Year-Old. And I knew by her air of rapt detachment, that she was re-living the time she had ridden for the last time over that same threshold on her Father's back. The two had stood in the spill of light while the sun struck sparks of gold from the Navy Braid. Coming out of her recollections, Roberta saith unto me dreamily, My curls caught in the Shine on his shoulder.

These well-guarded memories might have remained inviolate, had there not come the inevitable day when a Literal Lad could hold his peace no longer. With the thoughtless Cruelty of Youth spake he before all, saying, Roberta, dost thou not know the truth concerning thy Father?

Then as I sought desperately for some kindly way in which to soften the Blow, the Little Maiden herself did answer quietly, I do understand. My Daddy was Missing for many days. And when he was found, he was in Heaven.

Here, for a moment, fell I to day-dreaming. I wished that Roberta's comforting words might become Official. Yea, that the War Department might wire them unto all Gold Star Mothers. And lo, my dreaming was shattered by more information from the Literal Lad. This time, he was explaining with the candour of all of his six summers, Roberta, thou dost not need to pray longer for one who is already in Heaven.

My little Maiden remained unruffled by this last thrust. Keeping her eyes on the shimmering light of the doorway, she answered with a hopeful inflection: I know. But I thought it might help to keep him in Good Shape.

Now I am ignorant concerning the degrees of Happiness in Paradise. And perchance I may be accounted an Heretic. Yet believe I that a certain young Naval Officer is enjoying an especial Portion of Heavenly Bliss—and all because of the faith· ful petitions of his little Roberta.

WHEN THE SAP IS UP

*Y*ESTERDAY, competed I with Spring. In the morn the Children were Volcanoes of Noise. Doors slammed, and marbles rolled to the floor. There was a ceaseless chirping like unto the birds, yea, and a constant tugging at the buckles and laces of imprisoning Shoes. While seemingly for Encouragement, ever and anon there sounded the high note of a fresh-cut but well-concealed Willow Whistle.

Albeit when the Wind idled, my Little Ones were possessed of the same Inertia. Finally, the last fitful Breeze went over the hill. And they sank back dreamily, their voices taking on a droning quality like the hum of insects in the new grass.

As the slow hours ticked away, I caught the Infection. Stifling a yawn I thought wearily, Why try to Inoculate Knowledge into such Non-conformists? Then suddenly sensed I an absence of the usual tappings of Toes as of drum-beats, and the scrapings of Heels like distant thunder. And I caught the audible whisper, Sharleen, why not turn them out to graze? Then looked I, and behold, every foot in the room was unshod save those of the aforesaid Maiden. And from her discomforted countenance I saw that she endured the Pains of Pride only because for the first time, she wore Dancing Slippers of silver braid.

Moreover, I guessed that this Mischief had been wrought during my brief absence in the Principal's Office. Wherefore searched I diligently for the Hidden Cache. And lo, mine eyes suddenly lighted upon rows of Sandals and Slippers placed neatly side by side beneath mine own table! There were divers kinds: the squeaky new ones, the scuffed and elegant, yea, even those that had sprung a Leak—and all did bear, in some unique fashion, the Contour of the Owner. Then suddenly, against my will, but with inward Pride, I was minded that like the Dove of Noah, each Foot had returned to its Ark of Safety.

However, being a Teacher, I was likewise filled with Compunction. So I rebuked the Children, saying, In two minutes when the bell for dismissal ringeth, get you up every one of you and don your Shoes. Moreover, pause not, neither to the right nor the left, till ye reach your Abodes. And hearken well! No foot in this room shall tomorrow go unshod save with a Parent's Permission.

Then gat they all up with Circumspection and did as I had commanded. But I remembered the Vagrant Spring Yearnings of mine own Childhood. And I guessed their future Intents. So repaired I unto a Window.

Now a huge Boulder reclined by one side of the road which my Pupils needs must travel. On the other stretched a long grassy Incline. Between, within a sunken place of the Pavement, there lay a Pool of clear Rain Water.

And lo, even as I had surmised, the first Lad when he reached the Boulder, sat upon it and removed his Shoes. In like manner did they all. The tiny Maiden, Sharleen, was the last. And as she arose, she held high the Silver Dancing Shoes for protection against her breast.

Then said I consolingly within myself, Thus have such things ever been. Moreover, if the Tides and Sun, yea, and all Nature feel this Resurgence, why not the exuberant heart of a Child? And for one fleeting moment mused I sorrowfully upon the hordes of Enslaved Children trudging the highways of Other Lands. And I said exultantly, These are Free!

And I gazed thankfully above the Incline where the air was full of bird cries. Then lowering mine eyes I watched through a shining blur my Little Ones cross the pavement and dance in High-handed Fashion within the sparkling Pool. Once there sounded a clear, insistent note from the recovered Willow Whistle. Then with the Spring Wind blowing grass blades between their toes, my Children, with one accord, went racing up the April Hill!

EASTER FIASCO

My Six-Year-Olds respond with due reverence unto the Resurrection Story. But being Mimics of Adults, they likewise lift their voices high in praise of the Easter Parade.

Thus, one Spring morning when white clouds drifted across the blue, the Children of one accord besought me that they be permitted, for one day, to wear their Easter Apparel unto school. And I, in ignorance, consented.

And behold, on Good Friday, my schoolroom did shimmer with the iridescence of a rainbow. Tiny Lads, uncomfortably neat in colored Spring suits, were further embellished with bowties of flaming hue. The Damsels were a maze of pastel ruffles and sashes, their crowns of femininity being the delicate, feathery bonnets encircling blonde or brunette curls.

It was during this innocent worship unto the god of Fashion that a rural bus arrived, depositing my Two Tardies.

The first, Jimmy Joe, made an auspicious entrance, walking in proud consciousness of his Hat. The headpiece in question was a broad-brimmed felt fashioned after the similitude of a man's. Save that at one side it was decorated with a speckled feather of green.

Unaware that he had startled his classmates, my Lad walked to his accustomed seat, the Hat tilted in debonair manner over one ear. And he sat down in the pure joy of being admired and envied. Later being admonished, he repaired with reluctance unto the cloakroom, hanging the Hat in lone glory amongst a score of leather Helmets decreed by Fashion.

Scarcely had the Children recovered from their shocked surprise over Jimmy Joe, when Lucinda paused by my side for Commendation. Her Easter costume was of stiff Upholstery material, the entire color scheme being a lifeless, leaden brown. For ornament, it had a deep chesty frill of the same around the neck. And the full skirt swinging almost ankle-length may best be described by the word Whirl.

Gazing thereon, I sought feverishly for some discreet saying with which to explain away its ugliness. Then out of the painful silence, heard I the voice of the Maiden herself, saying pridefully, My Mother made this Dress from some Seat Covers. Then did I despair utterly. For well I knew that the words were fatal. And indeed the whole Assemblage did gaze upon her anew with open-mouthed Astonishment. But Lucinda's estate being far from that of a Moron, she lifted eloquent brown eyes in puzzled questioning. Then sensing the amazement, yea, and the held-in Laughter, she took her seat in Abasement. Now, within a small circle of the Elect, sat a Fortune-favored Maiden named Eunice. And albeit she was possessed of many riches, yet was she ever concerned for the Unfortunate. Swiftly did she move to the place where Lucinda was submerged with Humiliation. And she saith in a clear voice for the Ears of the Class: Lucinda, with thy large brown eyes and thy matching Easter Dress, thou art the only one who dost resemble a beautiful Woods Fairy. And lo, a tremulous smile broke over the face of Lucinda. And she was half-comforted.

But alas, the end of the Easter Misadventure was not yet. At recess, Jimmy Joe ran unto me, his new Hat demolished within his hands. And he saith in the incredulous tones of the Newly-hurt, A big boy did jerk off mine Hat and throw it in the dust, calling me a Guinea Feather.

Now, that night I smarted long with Indignation. And in the privacy of mine own room, did I ask forgiveness for my part in the innocent Tragedy of Errors. Moreover, I was persuaded that if Lucinda's Dress had only possessed the label, Original—yea, or some such inscription as Country Quaint, it would have been loudly acclaimed by the Rich and Fashionable. For verily, when Calico goeth Urban, the status of its Wearer changeth it into many subtle Forms.

Likewise, since sleep had forsaken mine eyelids, I moralized further, saying, Would that the Human Race were freed from the ever-changing influence of Fashion and Taste. Then might I never again be a shamed Witness to the Sensitive Spirits quivering beneath a Seat-Covers Dress or a Guinea-Feather Hat!

RATIONING

*S*HE was newly come unto our school. On a snowy Winter's day, her Big Brother lifted her from the Automobile onto his shoulders. Proudly he carried her thus, putting her gently down upon the school threshold as if she were a Crown Jewel.

And she was richly appareled. Still do I remember the white Snow-suit. Yea, and the gleaming fur Muff and Mittens. A snowy Cap sat upon her black curls, while from her neck hung a tiny Coin Purse of the same softness. Verily, as I gazed upon the delicate features and shining hair, Lila appeared unto me the exact reproduction of a Fairy-Story Princess. Yet for this very cause, mayhap, had she been shielded from the Hardships of Life. And she did still maintain the Innocence of Babyhood. Especially where I was concerned. For unto the little Maiden the words of a Teacher were Omnipotent.

Now, it transpired later when the Spring returned, and the orchards were blowing pink and white, that I recited at Story Hour the delectable poem, The Sugar Plum Tree. And all the while, Lila did gaze upon me with her naïve Air of Unquestioning Trust. And with misgivings saw I that as she heard, she

Believed. Yet she waited patiently until I was finished. Then raising her great dark eyes, she saith hopefully, Hast thou ever planted any Sugar Plum Trees?

Now, I dreaded to see the Chrysalis of her Faith so rudely shattered. Hence answered I evasively, Nay, as yet have I neither planted nor seen one of these Sugar Plum Trees. And there I hoped the Matter rested.

A fortnight later, my Grade and I did celebrate that Pagan Rite known as an Easter-egg Hunt. And on the aforesaid day, Lila was absent from school. Wherefore said I unto the other Children, This thing will I do: Until Lila's return I will place her bag of Candy Eggs upon the highest shelf. See ye unto it that I am duly reminded.

Then did my Little Ones agree with alacrity. Verily, for the four and three days of the Damsel's absence they did guard the Cellophane Package with greedy eyes. And on the day of her return, one small Informer betrayed all to her concerning the Eggs before she had crossed the threshold. And her comely little countenance registered Great Expectations.

Thereafter, it did transpire daily that when the Eggs came to my remembrance, it seemed too soon after Breakfast Hour, or too nigh unto Lunch Time. And all the while, little Lila, too gently reared to remind me of broken promises, did look upon the transparent bag and its tantalizing contents with Longing. At length, when she could withstand Temptation no longer, she inclined her head in delicate manner toward the Freighted Argosy, saying with great tactfulness,

I see that thou art letting them go to Seed!

Then I, shamefacedly, did bestow upon the Child her Eggs. And perchance because of their iridescent coloring, she who ever dined sumptuously at home, did eat of the stale Aftermaths of Easter as though they were Manna.

And I confessed unto myself, saying, How numberless have been my Good Intentions lying unused because they awaited some Bigger Occasion. Moreover, resolved I never again through Over-Caution to send my pupils away Empty.

SHOE-SOLE TEA

Own the sandy wagon road walked we together: I and the School Nurse. Over us arched a roof of trees delicately hung with scarlet Trumpet Vine and Yellow Jessamine. And ever and anon as the road grew narrower, blossoms of the Crab Apple and Wild Plum drifted down upon us.

The Nurse was the first to break the magical silence. What of this Swamp Child? questioned she professionally. And I answered, She misseth several school days within the space of a week. And all of this because her whole Being is one Leaven of Superstition.

Perhaps we too will be Hexed, predicted my companion hopefully. For the Nurse, having once been a Missionary in Strange Lands, did still like to see the Commonplace kindled by Adventure and Romance.

While she yet spake, the wagon road appeared to dip abruptly. Yea, and the forest to change into Swampland. Ahead, in a clearing sprawled a cabin. From its sagging rafters hung all manner of Herbs for Healing Potions. And in the midst of these Simples, did stand a thin, sallow Woman, who for lifeless inertia resembled nothing so much as a dark String.

{ 78

By now were my knees shaking uncontrollably. But managed I in firm voice, Art thou the Mother of Sally Bell? And the Woman answered in a tone as monotonous as her countenance, Shore is! Then continued I, We are come hither, the School Nurse and I, because we yearn for the Well-being of thy little Damsel.

Then began the Mother of Sally Bell to unburden herself. That Young-un's pore feelin's wuz a puzzlement to me, she saith tonelessly, till I read the Ashes this mornin'. Then I put her comfortable inside a Horse Collar. And I brewed her a cup of Shoe-Sole Tea. Hit's agreein', she ended proudly. But hit would pleasure me did you take a look.

Tiptoeing into the one room of the cabin, we beheld Sally Bell on a corner pallet. Her head and shoulders were loosely encircled by an Ancient Horse Collar.

The Nurse moved swiftly unto the place where the little Damsel was. And she gave me an assuring wink, signifying that Sally Bell had survived the Bacterial Potion. Yea, and in spite of her Fetters, was sleeping peacefully.

Then spake I with purpose, saying, This Nurse possesseth much Knowledge, having ministered unto the Sick of many lands.

And the Mother of Sally Bell gazed at the immaculate Uniform. And she sensed the Cosmopolitan Experiences of its wearer. Therefore saith she in unique fashion: Yes, she's got Shoes and Been About! And she ended with a listless shake of her head, But you-uns and me can't be agreein'. You see, I holds with Charms and Spells.

The School Nurse squared her shoulders. Refusing to be ignored, she prescribed in professional tones, Please continue the Horse-Collar Treatment until morning. But cease all further dosages of Shoe-Sole Tea.

In such Imperious Fashion departed we from the gloomy Marshland with its greater Darkness of Superstition. As we gained higher ground, behold the sheen of sunset lay on the palmetto thickets. And it gilded the crests of the pines and glimmering dogwoods.

Here the Nurse did draw a long, relieved breath. That visit, saith she, was worse than many in the Blackness of the Congo. Here, it is doubly shameful, in that such Ignorance doth abound within a few furlongs of Knowledge and Culture. However, ended she blithely, let us slacken our pace and soften the experience with this Carolina Sunset.

Nay, I answered, I needs must hurry. Today, on Sally Bell's report card, I did with good conscience put a Zero in the space marked, Effort. But now, when I consider how she hath been reared within the confines of an Horse Collar, and nurtured on Shoe-Sole Tea, I am hastening to erase the Zero and inscribe an A.

NEVER SAY FAIL

*H*e was a handsome, ingenious little Lad with disarming eyes fringed with long curling lashes. And he thought highly of himself, yet without Obnoxiousness.

Now I have no objection to Confident Children. Yea, I prefer them to Nonsense-Makers who twitch foreheads and ears to induce Laughter. Or to Over-Shy Little Ones who continually droop with Inferiority, begging for Clemency.

And Walter radiated Assurance. Inflating his vanity was the knowledge that he possessed a dashing, much Be-ribboned Father lately home from the Wars. And a Great-Aunt who wore with poise and distinction the Regalia of a Colonial Dame.

Thus it occurred to me that it might enliven the day (and not harm Walter) to further test his Confidence. For lo, there was a baffling Enigma in the Spelling Lesson. Our usual procedure of following the spelling of words with simple, original sentences, seemed doomed. The two new words: AM and ME, would not reasonably reside together. And the Children had an obsession for fitting them jig-saw fashion, thus forcing them to conform.

Thinking to dodge the Issue personally, I challenged anyone to Solve the Insolvable. After a few mental efforts, the rest of the class subsided in Bafflement. But Walter was a Determined Soul. He surveyed the Words without hesitation or trepidation. Then with a regal nod of the head, he produced this sentence—which, though Ungrammatical, was a Model in Brevity and allowable Self-esteem:

I AM ME!

CASEKNIFE

My first sight of Stanley was against a desolate expanse of Marshland with its accompanying Backdrop of swaying Spanish Moss. And something in the way the disreputably clad Lad straightened and lifted his ragged palmetto hat, assured me that he was no true Product of the Piney Woods.

My curiosity was furthered on the morrow when I found him numbered amongst my First Grade Pupils. And though he presented himself in tattered raiment, the Surname which he gave did rival the Proudest in the State.

Wherefore, sought I out an elderly Teacher of Irreproachable Descent. And I ventured a cautious inquiry concerning this extraordinary Child.

At first, the French Huguenot Teacher did close her lips in a thin straight line. For although she knew the Social Status of everyone in the Region round about, she resented revealing it to an Outsider. Yea, her stately figure did stiffen as she saith with chilling asperity the single word, Why?

Then answered I bravely, Unless I err greatly, this Lad of French Lineage is as one marooned in this Primeval World where he finds himself. Yea, and he yearneth with half-understood longings for his Rightful Planet.

Then did some of the iciness of the French Huguenot Teacher dissolve. Yet her voice was still the voice of a Gossip Detester as she admitted, Thou hast guessed rightly. The Lad's Father was an Aristocrat. But he defied all the Common Decencies. In a drunken stupor he did marry an illiterate girl of the Piney Woods. Here the Narrator paused and sighed heavily. Well, ended she tartly, the man died two years ago. Today, the woman is a Sloven. And this Child is the Dividend of their Folly.

Though the Father be only a Shadowy Background, pronounced I boldly, yet am I sure that this Lad of the fine proud face doth Hark Back. Perhaps I can help to reclaim him. At any rate, it will prove intriguing to teach one whose Ancestors are so continually Nudging him.

Now, this was no idle boast concerning the Pull of Paternity. For behold, on a winter's day when I brought into the schoolroom a bouquet of hothouse flowers, Stanley did ask the name of the blossoms. When I answered, Daffodils, then did his dark eyes deepen and sparkle. And he quoted gropingly as though feeling for long-misplaced words,

And then my heart with pleasure fills,
And dances with the daffodils.

As I looked upon him in Astonishment, I saw that his happy little face shone as though he had been touched by a Wand. And he explained with dignity, Ma can't read. But my Pa, he had larnin' and taught me rimes. Some, ended he soberly, were not happy. We called them Sniff Poems.

Say a Sniff one, I implored. Then gazing seriously at me with his eloquent dark eyes the Lad recited,

The day is cold, and dark, and dreary;
It rains, and the wind is never weary . . . . . .

But here I interrupted with utter incongruity, Doth not thy
Mother sell eggs?

And Stanley, relapsing into his backwoods vernacular, made
answer, When the hens Oblige.

Tomorrow, then, saith I triumphantly, will be Saturday.
Perhaps thou canst bring me eggs very early in the morning.

And lo, on the morrow, stood Stan at mine apartment door
lacing his slender fingers together in apology for his dearth of
eggs.

Wherefore confessed I outright, saying, I asked thee because
I am a lonely person. And I planned that we have breakfast
together.

It's not fitten, spake Stan wistfully. I have not rubbed up
enough. Then suddenly he seemed to reconsider, and quietly
asserting his position, did take his place at the table.

After the saying of Grace, the Lad took up his knife and fork.
Then, as quickly, laid both down. Seeing that Panic had
touched him, I neither spake nor moved. Soon with a grim
Determination picked he up one of the Offending Members
again. And he ran his fingers appreciatively along its engraved
handle. Then he affirmed seriously, I have helt a Caseknife
before, but I can't seem to unwrastle the ways of it. My Pa,
he explained, was a ready hand with a Knife and Fork, but when
he died, our using of them petered out. Still holding tenaciously
to the baffling instrument, he ended, When I started to school
last year we had just one Knife left. Then one day the dog hid it
in the yard.

For the space of two hours listened I to the uncouth speech of the Piney Woods sprinkled with underlying tones and expressions of Gentility. And at last, as I watched his straight little back receding through the clear light of the morning, I was minded of the words of our Ethiopian Janitor, De odder Chilluns has some clothes and money, but dat boy Stan, he's got de Shine!

Now, behold, I spake of all these things again unto the French Huguenot Teacher. And I boasted, Stanley hath stored back within him Sensitivities and Discriminations as discernible as others' inherited eyes or noses. And I ended recklessly, If a Teacher could deposit a Child upon boardinghouse keepers, then would I be tempted to adopt the Lad. Nevertheless, will I make this request: That when I am old and leaning on a staff, thou wilt mail unto the address I shall then send you, the true Sequel of Stanley.

To this the Teacher made no agreement. But she spake a little unsteadily, saying, I have wrestled with my Conscience all year concerning this Child. And it hath told me that nothing Good is ever lost. So mayhap thou art right. Perhaps it will take more than one Prodigal Father's lifetime and his Boy's seven short years of impoverishment and neglect to destroy the Culture it took generations to perfect. Nevertheless, ended she in a disillusioned tone, it will also take a Miracle to produce the Blossom thou expectest from such Untoward Soil.

Now, every Teacher liveth on a Diet of Surprises. And behold, on the day I left that Region, happened the very Miracle of which my Friend had spoken so scornfully. For lo, she and little Stanley did approach me hand-in-hand together. And for the first time the voice of the French Huguenot Teacher had a

Personal Ring. Thou needest have no fear concerning the Sequel, saith she in a rush of emotion. Then abandoning all pretenses she added, Stanley's Father was the son of my married Sister. And what she hath, in Wounded Pride, withheld from this Lad, she and I will now jointly undertake.

All the while she was speaking, was she unrolling a package containing a Knife of silver bearing an imposing Crest. This, handed she to Stanley to give unto me. A Token, explained she in a tone of forced lightness, that not only shall our Lad have every chance to bear the name of his Forefathers proudly, but in deference to you, shall he learn to Unwrastle all the intricacies of the Fork and Knife.

THE DOTS HAVE IT

HOUGH the Earth rock and swell, yea, and though there be Wars and rumours of Wars, yet when Children draw, Dots and Circles will always be in the Ascendancy. These whimsical Circular Curlicues never become outmoded. Verily, whenever I see Cow-licks, Top-knots, or Love-curls bent over a sheet of drawing paper, then know I that Dots are Indicated.

Thus, on a Spring day, knew I by the contented humming as of bees around an hive, that the output of these scrawled Ovals would be Liberal. Being indifferent to this generosity, I suggested that the Idle Section of my grade draw the Old Oaken Bucket. Now, during a Unit on Water I had often read this ancient poem. For Children revel in its Antiquity.

And immediately, Patsy proceeded to obey. Remembering her phenomenal memory, I knew that in Powers of Execution, she would leave nothing to be desired. Falling into the Swing of Things, she swished her hair into the air. Then began she a series of Round-about Motions. And by the Curve of Concentration on her lips, I could literally feel the twists and twirls of her Rhythmic Rings. At last when the masterpiece was revealed, I beheld scores and scores of Bubbly-looking Balls— all suspended by a spidery trail of lines encircling and protecting the entire scene. Whereupon, questioned I the little Damsel sharply, saying, Wherefore upon a well and bucket do you place hundreds of Circles and Dots?

Patsy gazed upon me pityingly. Then said she in an adult tone of retrospection, Those are the Loved Spots which my Infancy Knew.

A fortnight later, David, mine Original Pupil, asked a question which was a natural progression in our History of Dots. His fellow-classman had broken a leg on the playground. For days, the accident intruded itself within and without all Discussion Periods. Finally, I unwittingly added fuel unto the fire by contributing thus: Children, an interesting thing hath developed upon our Lad's X-ray plate. His leg is broken in exactly the Shape of a Question Mark.

David waved his hand excitedly. Then asked he in one breathless rush, Did the Dot below it show, too?

Understand, I know not the Symbolism of Dots. Yet over this one thing am I constantly amazed: How these Tiny Architects can instantly furnish a Reasonable Alibi for their Circular Constructions. Horace, for example, when told to draw Something, did with stupendous mental effort and many twistings of the head and rollings of the tongue, concoct a likeness of his Teacher. Then, as a postscript, added he with Telling Effect three gigantic Round Adornments on my blouse front. For this admonished I him bluntly, saying, If thou must imagine Buttons where none reside, thou couldest at least have put them in a straight row.

They are not Buttons, quoth Horace, wrinkling his nose with an instant's reflection. They are the three Biscuits you ate for Breakfast.

{ 90

COME IN, MAGIC

ODAY, after my Little Ones were dismissed, Spring, by a strange Alchemy of sunlight and plum blossoms, did transform a prosaic school window into the shimmering splendour of Baghdad and Babylon. In such glamorous atmosphere I could no longer pretend to work. Hence, found I myself, as I do even now, reliving an ancient Game of my First Graders.

It is a thrilling Drama of Suspense, climaxed by marvelous Discovery. Yet it runneth simply enough. A Child chosen as Guesser repaireth beyond an outer door. Then someone within the room toucheth an Object. And behold, when the Guesser is recalled, he miraculously can tell exactly what was Touched.

Now the Children understand the Code. They know that when I catechize the Guesser, the object touched will be the one I mention immediately following one possessing the color of Green. Yet this simple Ruse, even when fully explained and comprehended, still remaineth little short of Sorcery. Mayhap this is why, years ago, as my suddenly sobered Frolickers gazed with Awe at the door from which the Magician would emerge, that one Marilyn, a veritable Bundle of Curls and Whimsy, did over-rule my literal call. With stars in her eyes she bade the

Closeted One to re-enter by clapping her hands and crying ecstatically, Come in, Magic!

In such manner, her enticing Signal did become Universal. Henceforth, the Game so prosaically known for generations as Greeny, was transformed by this magic Password into a sort of Glorified Pageantry. Yea, and for this oft-requested Drama, I possess ever a Star-spangled Cast. One that needs no Scenery or Props. For children live in Enchanted Territory, and are never reduced to the things which can merely be seen or handled.

Wherefore, today as I sat in my deserted schoolroom, I did find myself envying Marilyn and her Kind their ready belief in Foreknowledge. Yea, in all such things as Lucky Pennies, and Wishes on the Moon. Even of Dandelions Tickled under the Chin. For I remember that before we became Jaded Adults, we also owned Marilyn's rose-coloured glasses. And I was silent, remembering that often the pregnant Stillness of a room hath something momentous to say. . . . . .

And behold, as I tarried, a series of Flash-backs did crystallize within a few instants the meaning of all my school years. As I reached back into the Past, I could hear Allan showering his Golden Litany down the hospital ward. And I also beheld Clara. Audacious Clara, her little chin high, her confident eyes peering beyond the ice-rimmed window for the Miracle of a Tardy Santa Claus. With like clarity, I re-visualized the Imaginary Adventures of the little Ananias which actually ended in Heroic Splendour on his Be-medalled Chest. Last of all, saw I Daniel, once the hungry-hearted, but now racing through the Springtide as happily as a Knight in Plumes and Cloth-of-Gold.

Then an inner Voice spake, declaring, Now thou seest that there still be Fairy-Facts. Yea, that Make-Believes may yet come true. These still lie within all of us, and may be recalled if only we have the Shining Faith of a Child to bring them again unto Resurrection.

And lo, after the Voice had receded, I did feel lifted from the rut of Dull and Tedious Teaching. Yea, at this very moment am I still possessed of that heady, intoxicated sensation. Furthermore, believe I that if ever I do Inherit Eternity that my Children will be there, just beyond the Enchanted Door, awaiting The Great Magician. And that when He doth appear, then shall we behold the greatest Magic of all: The Miracle of Immortality!

ALICE LEE HUMPHREYS, author of *Heaven in My Hand, Angels in Pinafores,* and *Three Hear the Bells,* was born in the tiny rural town of Donalds, South Carolina. While still a young girl, she went to live with an aunt in nearby Due West. There she was educated in the preparatory department of the Woman's College (now Erskine College). She also holds a Master's degree from the school.

Twenty-six of Miss Humphreys' thirty-nine years as a first-grade teacher were spent at Kennedy Street School, Anderson, South Carolina. Earlier she taught in Rock Hill, Pelzer, and Level Land, South Carolina, and Biltmore, North Carolina. Now retired, she lives in Honea Path, South Carolina.

Her three books were written, she says, "to inspire humdrum parents and teachers to catch the fresh, exciting quality of children." Most of her characters were drawn from her teaching experiences in Anderson. When the city proclaimed "Alice Lee Humphreys Day" some years ago, the mayor commented: "Here Miss Humphreys has seen the children who have laughed, wept, and danced through the pages of her books, and it is in Anderson that she has satisfied her desire to write. Miss Humphreys has received national acclaim through the medium of [her] fine books, but she is first and foremost a school teacher."